CENGAGE Learning

Drama for Students, Volume 2

Staff

David Galens and Lynn M. Spampinato, *Editors*

Thomas Allbaugh, Craig Bentley, Terry Browne, Christopher Busiel, Stephen Coy, L. M. Domina, John Fiero, Carol L. Hamilton, Erika Kreger, Jennifer Lewin, Sheri Metzger, Daniel Moran, Terry Nienhuis, Bonnie Russell, Arnold Schmidt, William Wiles, Joanne Woolway, *Contributing Writers*

Elizabeth Cranston, Kathleen J. Edgar, Joshua Kondek, Marie Lazzari, Tom Ligotti, Marie Napierkowski, Scot Peacock, Mary Ruby, Diane Telgen, Patti Tippett, Kathleen Wilson, Pam Zuber, *Contributing Editors*

Pamela Wilwerth Aue, *Managing Editor*

Jeffery Chapman, *Programmer/Analyst*

Victoria B. Cariappa, *Research Team Manager*
Michele P. LaMeau, Andy Guy Malonis, Barb

McNeil, Gary Oudersluys, Maureen Richards, *Research Specialists*

Julia C. Daniel, Tamara C. Nott, Tracie A. Richardson, Cheryl L. Warnock, *Research Associates*

Susan M. Trosky, *Permissions Manager*
Kimberly F. Smilay, *Permissions Specialist*
Sarah Chesney, *Permissions Associate*
Steve Cusack, Kelly A. Quin, *Permissions Assistants*

Mary Beth Trimper, *Production Director*
Evi Seoud, *Assistant Production Manager*
Shanna Heilveil, *Production Assistant*

Randy Bassett, *Image Database Supervisor*
Mikal Ansari, Robert Duncan, *Imaging Specialists*
Pamela A. Reed, *Photography Coordinator*

Cynthia Baldwin, *Product Design Manager*
Cover design: Michelle DiMercurio, *Art Director*
Page design: Pamela A. E. Galbreath, *Senior Art Director*

Copyright © 1998
Gale Research
835 Penobscot Building
645 Griswold St.
Detroit, MI 48226-4094

ISBN 0-7876-1684-2

ISSN applied for and pending

Printed in the United States of America
10 9 8 7 6 5 4 3

Waiting for Godot

Samuel Beckett

1952

Introduction

Though difficult and sometimes baffling to read or (even) view, *Waiting for Godot* is nonetheless one of the most important works of our time. It revolutionized theatre in the twentieth century and had a profound influence on generations of succeeding dramatists, including such renowned contemporary playwrights as Harold Pinter and Tom Stoppard. After the appearance of *Waiting for Godot,* theatre was opened to possibilities that playwrights and audiences had never before imagined.

Initially written in French in 1948 as *En Attendant Godot,* Beckett's play was published in French in October of 1952 before its first stage production in Paris in January of 1953. Later translated into English by Beckett himself as *Waiting for Godot,* the play was produced in London in 1955 and in the United States in 1956 and has been produced worldwide. Beckett's play came to be considered an essential example of what Martin Esslin later called "Theatre of the Absurd," a term that Beckett disavowed but which remains a handy description for one of the most important theatre movements of the twentieth century.

"Absurdist Theatre" discards traditional plot, characters, and action to assault its audience with a disorienting experience. Characters often engage in seemingly meaningless dialogue or activities, and, as a result, the audience senses what it is like to live in a universe that doesn't "make sense." Beckett and others who adopted this style felt that this disoriented feeling was a more honest response to the post World War II world than the traditional belief in a rationally ordered universe. *Waiting for Godot* remains the most famous example of this form of drama.

Author Biography

Samuel Beckett was born near Dublin, Ireland, on April 13, 1906. During his school years he was more interested in athletics than in academics, but he became excited about the study of French and Italian near the middle of his university career at Trinity College, Dublin, and ultimately graduated with honors in December, 1927. After graduation Beckett attempted to teach school but found teaching very unpleasant. He then sought to make his living as a writer but gained only modest success with his poetry, criticism, and prose during the 1930s and 1940s. However, at the end of 1948, as a diversion from his work on a novel, Beckett wrote *Waiting for Godot* in less than four months and the tremendous impact of this and subsequent plays in the 1950s turned him into an international celebrity. His monumental career as a playwright was born and it continued to overshadow his highly respected work as an experimental novelist.

In 1928, when Beckett had taken up residence in Paris as a school teacher, he met the great Irish short story writer and novelist James Joyce, author of *Dubliners, A Portrait of the Artist as a Young Man,* and *Ulysses.* For a number of years in the 1930s Beckett worked closely with the already famous Joyce as Joyce labored on his revolutionary masterpiece, *Finnegans Wake.* Joyce's erudition, esoteric word play, and elusiveness of meaning were qualities that Beckett was striving for in his own work, and when Beckett turned to drama as his major form of expression these aspects of his style intensified. *Waiting for Godot* stunned audiences with its bare set, unusual dialogue, slight plot, and bizarre characters, but subsequent plays became even more unusual. Throughout his writing career, Beckett was most interested in "minimalism," the attempt to create the greatest artistic effects with the least means possible. Beckett's plays got shorter and shorter until he eventually wrote a piece called *Breath* that lasted forty seconds and consisted of the sound of a single inhalation and exhalation of breath accompanying the rising and falling of the lights on a littered stage.

During World War II, Beckett lived in southern France and was active in the French Resistance, an underground movement fighting against the German occupation of France. Some have seen *Waiting for Godot* as a reflection on this period of Beckett's life. Beckett died of respiratory failure in Paris on December 22, 1989, and is considered by many to be one of the most innovative, daring, and revolutionary dramatists of the twentieth century. In 1969 he was awarded the Nobel Prize for Literature for "a body of work that, in new forms of fiction and the theatre, has transmuted the destitution of modern man into his exaltation."

Plot Summary

Act I

On a country road, at evening, near a tree with no leaves, a middle-aged man named Estragon (nicknamed Gogo) sits on a low mound struggling to remove his boots. He is soon joined by his friend, Vladimir (nicknamed Didi), who is glad to see him again and who recalls the story of the two thieves crucified with Christ and wonders whether it was true that one of them was chosen to be saved.

Estragon suggests that they leave this place but Vladimir reminds him they must stay because they are waiting for Mr. Godot. They debate whether this is the right place or time for their meeting, but their discussion tires Estragon and he falls asleep. After Vladimir wakes Estragon they decide that they might pass the time while they wait by hanging themselves, but the lone tree in sight seems too frail to hold them and they argue over who should hang himself first.

Two more characters enter—a man named Lucky, who carries a heavy load and has a rope around his neck, and a domineering man named Pozzo, who whips Lucky forward. The frightened Estragon and Vladimir huddle together and Estragon asks if Pozzo is Mr. Godot, but Pozzo, who claims to own the land they are on, intimidates Estragon and Vladimir into disavowing their connection with Godot. Pozzo proposes to stay with these two men and orders Lucky to provide what he needs to sit and relax. As Pozzo eats chicken, Estragon and Vladimir inspect Lucky; Estragon sees the chicken bones that Pozzo has thrown on the ground and is given permission to gnaw on them. Pozzo explains that he is taking Lucky to the fair to sell him, and when Lucky hears this he begins to weep, but when Estragon brings Lucky a handkerchief for his tears Lucky kicks Estragon violently in the shin.

Vladimir exits to urinate, and, after he returns, Pozzo asks if Estragon and Vladimir would like Lucky to entertain them by "thinking," but Lucky's thinking turns out to be a long, almost nonsensical monologue. Pozzo and Lucky announce their departure, do not move, but then finally manage to leave, and Vladimir and Estragon comment on how the visit from Pozzo and Lucky helped pass the time while they waited for Godot. Finally, a boy enters, addresses Vladimir as Mr. Albert, and delivers the message that Mr. Godot will not be coming this evening but will surely come tomorrow. After the boy leaves, Vladimir and Estragon also decide to leave but, after declaring their resolve, do not move.

Act II

The next day, at the same time and place (the tree now has four or five leaves), Vladimir enters in an agitated state and sings a circular kind of song about a dog. Estragon enters, feeling gloomy about the beating he reports he has suffered, and he and Vladimir agree to say that they are happy, though they do not appear to be. They rededicate themselves to waiting for Godot, and Estragon suggests they could pass the time by contradicting one another or by asking one another questions. After a number of diverting exchanges, Vladimir sees Lucky's hat, left from yesterday, and he and Estragon do a vaudeville "bit" exchanging hats until Vladimir throws his own on the ground. Vladimir suggests they pretend to be Pozzo and Lucky, which they do with limited success, but when the game sends Estragon offstage, he quickly returns, frantically announcing that "they" are coming. Vladimir thinks this means that Godot is coming but Estragon's fear finally overtakes Vladimir as well and they look for a place to hide. The tree offers little in the way of cover. Estragon calms down and suggests that they simply watch carefully. They then discover another game, calling one another names, and they insult one another until Estragon comes up with the ultimate insult, calling Vladimir a "critic." After this game ends, they explore other diversions until they are interrupted by another visit from Pozzo and Lucky.

On this visit, Pozzo is blind and bumps into Lucky after they enter, knocking them both down. Estragon asks if it is Godot who has arrived, but Vladimir is simply happy that they now have company as they wait for Godot. Pozzo is quite helpless, unable to get up from the ground, and Vladimir engages in a long philosophical discourse on whether he and Estragon should help Pozzo get up. In attempting to lift Pozzo, Vladimir falls himself and when Estragon attempts to help Vladimir up both end on the ground. With all three seated and unable to rise, Vladimir announces that "we've arrived. . . we are men." Vladimir and Estragon's next effort to rise is effortless and they help Pozzo to his feet, supporting him on each side. Pozzo begs them not to leave him. In response to Pozzo's question, "is it evening," Vladimir and Estragon scrutinize the sunset and conclude that they have indeed passed another day. Pozzo asks about Lucky, his "menial," who seems to be sleeping, and Estragon advances toward Lucky somewhat fearfully, remembering the kick in the shins he received the day before. For revenge, Estragon kicks the sleeping Lucky but hurts his foot in the process as Lucky awakes. Estragon sits and goes to sleep. Vladimir engages Pozzo in conversation and Pozzo claims no memory of a visit the day before. As Pozzo prepares to leave, Vladimir asks him what he does, blind, if he falls where no one is there to help him. Pozzo says, "we wait till we can get up. Then we go on." Vladimir asks if Pozzo will have Lucky sing or "think" again before they leave, but Pozzo reveals that Lucky is now "dumb," or mute, incapable of making sounds —"he can't even groan." Vladimir is confused because it seems to him that just yesterday Lucky could speak, but Pozzo is aggravated by the concept of time. For him, time is a meaningless concept; he says that the moments of our lives are like a light that "gleams an instant, then it's night once more." With those words, Pozzo and Lucky leave. Soon after they leave the stage, they fall down again.

Vladimir wakens Estragon, who is annoyed because he was dreaming that he was happy. Vladimir wonders how much of what he takes to be true is maybe some kind of dreaming. A boy enters, addressing Vladimir again as Mr. Albert, and announces that Godot will not be coming this evening but will be coming (without fail) tomorrow. The boy says he wasn't the one who came yesterday, though he seems to be to Vladimir. When Vladimir makes a sudden leap at the boy, the boy is frightened and runs off. Immediately, the sun sets, the moon rises, and Estragon awakes. Estragon talks of leaving but Vladimir reminds him they must wait for Godot to come tomorrow. They notice that everything is dead except the tree. They speculate again on the idea of hanging themselves but see that they lack a proper rope for it. When they try to use Estragon's belt for a rope, his pants fall down to his ankles. When they test the belt, it breaks. They decide that they can bring a stronger rope tomorrow. Vladimir says, "Well? Shall we go?" and Estragon ends the play by saying, "Yes, let's go." The final stage direction says, "They do not move."

Characters

Mr. Albert

See Vladimir

Boy

The messenger who arrives near the end of each act to inform Vladimir and Estragon that Mr. Godot will not arrive is simply called "boy." Timid and fearful, he addresses Vladimir as Mr. Albert and admits in the first act that Pozzo and his whip had frightened him and kept him from entering sooner. He claims that he tends goats for Mr. Godot and that Godot is good to him, though he admits that Godot beats the boy's brother. On each visit the boy claims to have not seen Vladimir and Estragon before. In the second act the boy reports that he thinks Godot has a white beard.

Media Adaptations

- A 1990 videotape production of *Waiting for Godot* is available from The Smithsonian Institution Press Video Division as part of a trilogy that includes productions of *Endgame* and *Krapp 's Last Tape.* Performed by the San Quentin Drama Workshop, the production of *Waiting for Godot* includes Rick Cluchey as Pozzo. Act I on the first tape lasts 77 minutes and Act II on the second tape lasts 60 minutes. The whole trilogy is presented under the title Beckett Directs Beckett but only because it is based on Beckett's original staging for theatre.

- The 1987 film *Weeds,* starring Nick Nolte, is based loosely on the experience of Rick Cluchey in San Quentin prison. Sentenced to life imprisonment without parole for kidnapping, robbery, and aggravated assault, Cluchey witnessed the famous San Quentin production of Beckett's play, became an actor, organized a prison drama group, and was eventually released after twelve years to become an accomplished interpreter of Beckett's characters on stage and in film.

- A 45-minute black and white version of Act II is available from Films for the Humanities (Princeton, NJ, 1988; orig. 1976) and features Zero Mostel, Burgess Meredith, and Milo O'Shea in a production directed by Alan Schneider, director of the ill-fated American premiere in Miami.

- A 50-minute lecture by Bert States entitled "*Waiting for Godot*: Speculations on Myth and Method," was recorded on audiocassette in 1976 by the Cornell Literature Forum.

- A 36-minute lecture on audiocassette by Kathryn Ludwigson entitled "Beckett's View of Man in *Waiting for Godot* and *Endgame*," was made in 1972 by

King's College. Part of a series entitled Christianity and Literature Cassettes, this lecture compares Beckett's description of modern man as lost and disoriented with the biblical view of man and points out passages in the dramas analogous to biblical texts.

- A 35-minute audiocassette program on the play by Lois Gordon as part of the Modern Drama Cassette Curriculum series was created in 1971 by Everett/Edwards of Deland, Florida.

- On June 26, 1961, a British television production of the play was broadcast with Peter Woodthorpe as Estragon and Jack MacGowran as Vladimir and directed by Donald McWhinnie. Beckett was not pleased with the production, feeling that the containment of the action in the small television frame misrepresented the drama of "small men locked in a big space."

- A 24-page musical score for a 10-minute performance entitled "Voices," based on the play, was published in 1960 by Universal Edition (London) and attributed to Marc Wilkinson. The score features a contralto voice singing in English and German and an instrumental ensemble of flute, clarinet, bass clarinet, and violoncello.

Didi

See Vladimir

Estragon (Es-tra-gon)

Estragon is one of the two men (often referred to as "tramps") who are waiting for Mr. Godot. He is the first to appear in the play and is more docile and timid than his friend Vladimir; Estragon usually follows Vladimir's lead. At times assertive, Estragon is more emotional and volatile than Vladimir but less engaged—he gives up more easily, does a lot of sleeping, likes to dream, and forgets more easily. He even forgets Godot's name at one point. He is confused more frequently than Vladimir and is more frequently afraid—perhaps because he is the one more often beaten and physically abused by others. He has bad feet, which hurt him in his too-small boots and which smell when hc has his boots off. He is more skeptical and questions more than Vladimir, doubts Godot more, and is more often anxious to leave or to travel separately from his friend. Estragon, along with Pozzo, does the eating in the play. If Estragon and Vladimir are Laurel and Hardy, Estragon is Stan Laurel, the skinny one who is frequently confused, frightened, and whiny.

Gogo

See Estragon

Lucky

Lucky is the miserable slave or "menial" whom Pozzo drives on stage in Act I and blindly follows in Act II, but while Pozzo's fortune and character changes Lucky's remains fairly similar. In the first act he is an abused beast of burden, an automaton carrying a huge load and suffering from neck abrasions where Pozzo violently jerks his halter. Lucky is understandably sad and quiet, but he is also loyal to Pozzo, eager to please, and violent himself when Estragon gets near enough to be kicked. His "thinking" seems full of a desperate energy that may come from an attempt to communicate his sadness. In the second act Lucky is mute and mostly sleeps. Lucky has long white hair that falls down around his face.

Pozzo (Po-dzo)

Pozzo is the bald, brutal, insensitive, and overbearing figure who intimidates Estragon and Vladimir in the first act of the play after he drives his "slave," Lucky, onto the scene. Pozzo is a sadistic bully with a large body and a huge voice who violently abuses Lucky, both physically and psychologically, forcing Lucky with whip and halter to serve his every whim and need. In the first act Pozzo seems wealthy, self-assured, and powerful. However, in the second act, Pozzo is blind and a much different person. He still has Lucky on a rope and calls him his "menial," but Pozzo now is timid, frightened, vulnerable, and helpless as he falls to the ground and cannot rise without assistance.

Vladimir (Vlad-eh-meer)

Vladimir is the more forceful, optimistic, and resilient of the two "tramps" waiting for Mr. Godot, but he is also sensitive, easily hurt, and quickly frustrated. He is extremely caring and protective of his friend, Estragon, and he more courageously expresses his outrage at Pozzo's mistreatment of Lucky. He usually leads Estragon in their games to "pass the time" and he initially represents the pair when strangers like Pozzo and the boy appear. Vladimir is the one most confident that Godot will appear and the most insistent that they meet their obligations by waiting. He is more of a thinker and philosopher than Estragon and he remembers the past much more clearly, though his memory frustrates him when other people don' t remember things the way he does. He sometimes becomes angry in these situations but occasionally doubts his own certainty. This more intellectual quality leads Vladimir to be more deeply brooding and gloomy but also more persistent than his friend. Vladimir has stinking breath and kidney problems. If Estragon and Vladimir are Laurel and Hardy,

Vladimir is Oliver Hardy, the fat one who does the "thinking" but is frequently dead wrong.

Themes

Human Condition

In this richly evocative "story" about two men who wait for another who never comes there are so many possible themes it is difficult to enumerate them. Those that are readily apparent include the issues of absurdity, alienation and loneliness, appearance and reality, death, doubt and ambiguity, time, the meaning of life, language and meaning, and the search for self. But one theme that encompasses many of these at once is the question of the human condition—who are we as humans and what is our short life on this planet really like?

We appear to be born without much awareness of our selves or our environment and as we mature to gradually acquire from the world around us a sense of identity and a concept of the universe. However, the concept of human life that we generally acquire may be fraught with illusions. Early in his life Beckett dismissed the Christian concept of God and based his concept of the human condition on the assumption that human existence ends in the grave, mat our most monumental achievements are insignificant measured by the cosmic scales of time and space, and that human life without illusions is generally difficult and sad. Vladimir and Estragon live in a world without comforting illusions about human dignity, the importance of work and achievement, the inevitability of justice, or the promise of an afterlife of eternal bliss. They live in a world where almost nothing is certain, where simply getting your boots off or sleeping through the night without having to urinate is a pretty significant achievement. They live in a world where violence and brutality can appear at any time, often victimizing them directly. They live without amenities, find joy in the smallest of victories, and are ultimately quite serious about their vague responsibility to wait for this mysterious figure who may or may not come and who may or may not reward them for their loyalty. It is a life lived on the razor's edge of hope and sadness.

Topics for Further Study

- Research the following three topics: the French Resistance during the German occupation of France in World War II, Beckett's personal role in that Resistance movement, and interpretations of *Waiting for Godot* that suggest Beckett is using the play to reflect on his war experience.

- Research the production of *Waiting for Godot* at San Quentin penitentiary in November of 1957 and discuss the conditions under which unsophisticated audiences can understand and respond enthusiastically to Beckett's play.

- Find places in the text of *Waiting for Godot* where the play is clearly funny. Then find places where the humor is less obvious but still quite rich. Finally, research the concept of "black humor" and describe the sense of humor that you find in *Waiting for Godot*.

- Research as many different productions of *Waiting for Godot* as you can and classify what these productions reveal about differences in presentation and interpretation. Then describe the features of a production that you would undertake.

- Compare the Existentialist and Christian interpretations of the play and decide which one seems to you more faithful to the text that Beckett wrote.

Strangely enough, Pozzo often voices most clearly what Beckett might have called the reality of this world. In Act I, for example, Estragon feels pity for the abused and weeping Lucky, who is sobbing because Pozzo has said aloud that he wants to "get rid of him." As Lucky sobs, Pozzo brutally says, "old dogs have more dignity." But when Estragon goes with a handkerchief to wipe his tears, Lucky kicks him violently in the shins and it is now Estragon in pain. Pozzo then offers this observation: "he's stopped crying. [To Estragon.] You have replaced him as it were. [Lyrically.] The tears of the world are a constant quantity. For each one who begins to weep, somewhere else another stops. The same is true of the laugh. [He laughs.] Let us not then speak ill of our generation, it is not any unhappier than its predecessors. [Pause.] Let us not speak well of it either. [Pause.] Let us not speak of it at all."

As Beckett dismissed what most of us take for granted, he eventually dismissed language itself as a reliable source of security. Ironically, this man of words ultimately mistrusted them. He knew that the word could never be counted on to convey meaning precisely and that linguistic meaning was always an approximation. Thus he shows Vladimir and Estragon spending most of their time dancing around words, attempting vainly to pin them down, to use them as guiding stars as best they can. At the end of the play, for example, Vladimir is struck by Estragon's suggestion that much of what Vladimir "knows" might be as unreliable as Estragon's dreams, and Vladimir launches into a poetic monologue that begins, "Was I sleeping, while the others suffered? Am I sleeping now?" But when he ends this lyrical moment of introspection he simply says, "what have I said?" This is a world where even words fail to wrestle our lives into consistently coherent patterns of meaning, a world where the human condition is radically insecure but where the struggle to find meaning is perhaps the only nobility left for us.

Friendship

It is tempting to see Beckett as a "nihilist," as someone who believed that there was nothing of value or meaning in human life, but the friendship of Estragon and Vladimir clearly offers us something positive and even uplifting in the difficult world of Beckett's play. In the unconventional banter of these two men it is sometimes easy to miss the intensity of their symbiotic relationship, but close attention to the theatrical qualities in their exchanges will show that they care deeply for one another and in many ways need one another to survive in their inhospitable world. Beckett, of course, is not sentimental about friendship—he is stubbornly realistic about everything he sees—but on the whole the relationship between Estragon and Vladimir is an important focus for understanding Beckett's most famous play.

In many places in the action Vladimir and Estragon bicker, misunderstand, and even ignore one another, but in other places their relationship is clearly tender, such as in the moment of Act II when Vladimir covers the sleeping Estragon with his coat. But if one were to focus on one moment in detail the most logical place to start might be the entrances of the two men at the beginning of the play. As the play begins, Estragon is sitting on a mound trying to take off his boot. Estragon and Vladimir have been separated overnight, but Beckett doesn't expect us to worry about why they have separated, any more than he expects us to give a moment's thought as to how they first met or how long they have known one another. It is enough to know that they are friends and that as the play begins Estragon is alone on this country road struggling to get his boots off. He finally gives up, saying "Nothing to be done," and at that moment Vladimir enters and responds to his friend's words as if he had been there from the start of Estragon's struggle—"I'm beginning to come round to that opinion," says Vladimir. The ease with which they are together again, as if they never were parted, is indicated deftly in die seamlessness of mat second line of the play. Vladimir then says, more directly, "I'm glad to see you back. I thought you were gone forever" and though the line is spoken casually the clear implication is that losing Estragon forever would have created a very considerable hole in Vladimir's life. Vladimir expresses concern over Estragon's beating, then quickly shifts into one of his annoyingly condescending roles as Estragon's protector. Vladimir talks, almost as if he simply enjoys hearing the sound of his own voice, while Estragon resumes the struggle with the boot. Eventually, Estragon succeeds in removing his boot and it could easily be suggested that he does so in part because of the mere presence of his friend. It is certainly no accident that just as Vladimir echoes Estragon's opening phrase, "Nothing to be done," Estragon "with a supreme effort succeeds in pulling off his boot." The removal of the boot, of course, is mundane. As Vladimir says, "Boots must be taken off every day." But in Beckett's careful art, the removal of the boot with the indirect emotional support of a friend is a metaphor for anything we attempt to do in our lives. In this life we face difficulties in the simple execution of daily affairs and ultimately we must face them alone or in the company of others who struggle as we do.

Style

Theatre of the Absurd

The seemingly endless waiting that Estragon and Vladimir undertake for the mysterious Godot has made Beckett's play one of the classic examples of what is called Theatre of the Absurd. The term refers both to its content—a bleak vision of the human condition—and to the style that expresses that vision. The idea that human life lacks meaning and purpose, that humans live in an indifferent or hostile universe, is frequently associated with Existentialist writers like the French philosophers Albert Camus (Kam-oo) and Jean-Paul Sartre (Sart). But when these two writers expounded their ideas in novels and plays, they generally used traditional literary techniques—that is, life-like characters; clear, linear plots; and conventional dialogue. But with writers like Beckett or the French dramatist Eugene Ionesco (E-on-es-co), the style is not an arbitrary choice but rather a necessary complement to the vision itself.

Beckett and those who adopted his style insisted that to effectively express the vision of absurdity one had to make the expression itself seem absurd. In other words, the audience had to experience what it felt like to live in an absurd world. Thus, the familiar and comforting qualities of a clear plot, realistic characters, plausible situations, and comprehensible dialogue had to be abandoned. In their place Beckett created a play where bizarre characters speak in what sometimes appears to be illogical, banal, chit chat and where events sometimes appear to change with no apparent logic. In *Waiting for Godot,* for example, this quality is embodied in its most extreme form in Lucky's first act monologue where he demonstrates his "thinking." For two full pages of text, Lucky goes on like this: "I resume alas alas on on in short in fine on on abode of stones who can doubt it I resume but not so fast I resume the skull to shrink."

Many of the play's original audience members and critics probably came to *Waiting for Godot* expecting something more traditional than Lucky's speech and were not able to adjust to what they were confronted with. Even today's reader may need a gentle reminder about expectations. As Hugh Kenner suggested at the outset of his book *A Reader's Guide to Samuel Beckett,* "the reader of Samuel Beckett may want a Guide chiefly to fortify him against irrelevant habits of attention, in particular the habit of reading 'for the story.'" For, as Martin Esslin explained in *The Theatre of the Absurd, "Waiting for Godot* does not tell a story; it explores a static situation. 'Nothing happens, nobody comes, nobody goes, it's awful.'" Or, as Kenner put it, "the substance of the play is waiting, amid uncertainty. . . . To wait; and to make the audience share the waiting; and to explicate the quality of the waiting: this is not to be done with 'plot.'"

Black Humor

Perhaps the easiest and also the most difficult thing to experience clearly in *Waiting for Godot* is its sense of humor. It's the easiest thing to experience because once one accepts the play on its own terms *Waiting for Godot* is wildly funny. But the play's humor is also the hardest thing to experience because the reputation of Beckett's play has created another set of expectations—that its dark vision must be taken with utmost seriousness.

However, a quick look at the subtitle of the play reveals that Beckett called it "a tragi-comedy in two acts," and this delicate balance between tragedy and comedy is probably the most essential ingredient in the play. Numerous critics have pointed out that *Waiting for Godot* is full of pratfalls, classic vaudeville "bits" like the wild swapping of hats in Act II, and the patter of comedians such as this from Act I:

> Estragon: [Anxious.]   And   we?
> Vladimir: I   beg   your   pardon?
> Estragon: I said, And we? Vladimir:
> I don't understand. Estragon: Where
> do we come in? Vladimir: Come in?
> Estragon: Take your time. Vladimir:
> Come in? On our hands and knees.
> Estragon: As bad as that?

Hugh Kenner has even discovered what appears to be a "source" for the farcical dropping of trousers that ends the play. He pointed out that in Laurel and Hardy's film *Way Out West* (1937) this dialogue occurs:

> Hardy: Get on the mule. Laurel: What? Hardy: Get *on* the mule.

At the end of *Waiting for Godot* we have:

> Vladimir: Pull on your trousers. Estragon: What? Vladimir: Pull on your trousers. Estragon: You want me to pull off my trousers? Vladimir: Pull ON your trousers. Estragon: [Realizing his trousers are down.] True. [He pulls up his trousers.]

Black Comedy is laughter that is generated by something truly painful. When we are led to laugh at tragedy or real suffering like death or the genuinely horrific, we are in the world of Black Comedy. In *Endgame* Nell says, "nothing is funnier than un-happiness." Beckett leads us to laugh because it may be the only viable response to extreme anxiety. In *Waiting for Godot,* of course, what follows the "trouser" passage above is the quite serious and even solemn concluding lines of the play—"they do not move."

The French Resistance Movement during World War II

Beckett wrote *Waiting for Godot* in the late months of 1948, three years after Allied forces had liberated France from German occupation, and some scholars suggest that his war experience might have served as an inspiration for the play. After German military forces had successfully invaded and occupied Northern France in the spring of 1940, a nominally free French government had been established in the South at Vichy and an underground French Resistance movement arose that attempted to frustrate and undermine German control of France. Beckett joined the Resistance movement in Paris in September of 1941 and helped pass secret information to England about German military movements. When an infiltrator began uncovering the names of Resistance members in Beckett's group, Beckett and his companion (later his wife) Suzanne had to flee Paris and travel into the South, where they eventually found refuge in the small village of Roussillon, near Avignon. In the French version of the play, this village is named as the place where Vladimir and Estragon picked grapes, an activity that Beckett and Suzanne actually engaged in. This has led some scholars to suggest that Vladimir and Estragon can, at least in part, represent Beckett and Suzanne in flight from Paris to Roussillon or the two of them waiting in an extremely dangerous form of exile for the war to end. In Roussillon, Beckett earned food and shelter by doing strenuous manual labor for local farmers, eventually working for a small local Resistance group, and trying to keep his identity hidden from the Germans occupying outlying areas. After the war, Beckett was awarded two French medals, the Croix de Guerre and the Medaille de la Reconnaissance, for his contributions to the war effort.

Compare & Contrast

- **1954:** Less than a decade after the U.S. military unleashed the frightening power of the atomic bomb in 1945, Russia and the United States began harnessing nuclear energy for peaceful uses. The first nuclear power station began producing electricity for Soviet industry and agriculture on June 27 at a station 55 miles from Moscow at Obninsk. In August, the U.S. Congress gave the approval for U.S. private industry to participate in the production of nuclear power.

  Today: The production of electricity through nuclear power plants has grown tremendously but has failed to become the dominant power source it was envisioned to be, in part because of the perceived dangers of nuclear power plants. Nuclear accidents at Three-Mile Island near Harrisburg, Pennsylvania, in 1979 and at Chernobyl near Kiev, Russia, in 1986 increased opposition to reliance on nuclear energy production.

- **1954:** Large corporations begin to use computers to facilitate business activities.

  Today: The world has been transformed by computers as they power and guide everything from wrist watches to space shuttles. The World Wide Web has virtually interconnected everyone on the globe by creating an "information super highway."

- **1954:** The first color television sets are introduced into the United States by RCA. Color reception is of unreliable quality but RCA will dominate the new market until 1959, when Zenith and others use the courts to challenge RCA's virtual monopoly.

  Today: The black and white

television is almost a collector's item and the transition is being made in the United States to the new digital television technology that will eventually make analog television sets obsolete. Digital television will provide a revolutionary clear image that delivers a "movie" quality picture.

- **1954:** Ray Kroc, a milkshake salesman in California, discovers a very successful but small California hamburger chain. He buys franchising rights from the owners, the McDonald brothers, and begins building his golden arches fast-food empire.

  Today: McDonald's is the largest fast-food chain in the world with nearly 20,000 restaurants in approximately 100 countries.

- **1954:** France asks the United States to help French troops surrounded at Dien Bien Phu in Indochina (Vietnam). President Eisenhower acknowledges the importance of containing Communist aggression in Southeast Asia but refuses to provide U.S. airpower to help relieve the siege.

  Today: The United States was

gradually drawn into the Vietnam conflict (while the French withdrew) until the United States under President Lyndon Johnson severely escalated U.S. involvement in the mid-1960s. Public anti-war sentiment ultimately forced American politicians to withdraw from the war without winning it militarily and the United States perhaps still suffers psychologically for its perceived defeat in the Vietnam.

Indeterminate Time and Place in Beckett's Play

More importantly for Beckett's art, however, is that *Waiting for Godot,* on the whole, clearly detaches itself from particular aspects of the historical and cultural context in which Beckett wrote in order to universalize the experience of Vladimir and Estragon. And it achieves this universal quality initially by placing the two figures in an indeterminate setting and time. As the play opens, the setting and time is simply described as "A country road. A tree. Evening." In the second act, the description is simply, "Next day. Same Time. Same Place." This backdrop is left unspecified in order to emphasize that the action of the play is a universal "situation" rather than a particular series of events that happened to a particular set of characters.

At one time in our century this waiting could have stood for South Africans waiting for apartheid to end in their native land. More than a half century after the unleashing of atomic energy, this waiting could still represent our fears of nuclear catastrophe. On a more personal level, many know what it is like to wait for news of a test for cancer. But all of these specific situations reveal how specificity can reduce the poetic evocativeness of Beckett's waiting to a mundane flatness. The unspecified nature of what Vladimir and Estragon wait for is what gives Beckett's play its extraordinary power.

The peculiar quality of Vladimir and Estragon's waiting, of course, is that they wait with only the vaguest sense of what they are waiting for and that they wait without much hope while still clinging to hope as their only ballast in an existential storm. But even this narrower description of the play's "waiting" leaves many possibilities for corresponding situations. For example, one of the most famous productions of *Waiting for Godot* perhaps reveals most clearly how the indeterminate time and place of the play permits it to speak to a wide variety of audience experiences. In *The Theatre of the Absurd* Martin Esslin examined the famous 1957 production of *Waiting for Godot* at San Quentin penitentiary. Prison officials had chosen Beckett's play largely because it had no women in it to distract the prisoners, but the San Francisco Actors' Workshop group that was performing the play was obviously concerned that such an arcane theatrical experience might baffle an audience of fourteen hundred convicts. Much to their surprise, however, the convicts understood the play immediately. One prisoner said, "Godot is society." Another said, "he's the outside." As Esslin reported, "a teacher at the prison was quoted as saying, 'they know what is meant by waiting . . . and they knew if Godot finally came, he would only be a disappointment.';" An article in the prison newspaper summarized the prisoners' response by saying, "We're still waiting for Godot, and shall continue to wait. When the scenery gets too drab and the action too slow, we'll call each other names and swear to part forever—but then, there's no place to go!" Esslin concluded that "it is said that Godot himself, as well as turns of phrase and characters from the play, have since become a permanent part of the private language, the institutional mythology of San Quentin." In 1961, one member of that convict audience, Rick Cluchey, helped form a group that produced seven productions of Beckett's plays for San Quentin audiences from 1961 to 1964. Cluchey later earned his release from San Quentin and had a distinguished career acting on stage and in films, especially as an interpreter of Beckett roles.

Critical Overview

After nearly a half-century, Beckett's *Waiting for Godot* remains one of the most important, respected, and powerful plays in the history of world theatre. Given its radically innovative style and great degree of difficulty, it is no surprise that audiences and critics have generally reacted to it in extremes—either of love or hate, admiration or disgust. Its original director, Roger Blin, recalled in an article in *Theater* that the reaction to the first production in January, 1953, in a small Paris theatre was "a sensation actually: wild applause broke out from some in the audience, others sat in baffled silence, fisticuffs were exchanged by pros and cons; most critics demolished play and production but a handful wrote prophetically."

Among those who wrote prophetically was the play's first reviewer, a relatively unknown critic named Sylvain Zegel, who proclaimed in a review in *Liberation* that the production was "an event which will be spoken of for a long time, and will be remembered years later." With amazing prescience, Zegel simply asserted that this first-time playwright "deserves comparison with the greatest." A more famous French critic at the time, Jacques Lemarchand, added an awareness of the play's dark humor, observing in *Figaro Litteraire* that *Waiting for Godot* "is also a funny play—sometimes very funny. The second night I was there the laughter was natural and unforced." He added that this humor "in no way diminished" the play's profound emotional intensity. Internationally acclaimed playwright Jean Anouilh (On-wee) was also one of *Waiting for Godot'* s early commentators and in *Arts Spectacles* simply proclaimed it "a masterpiece." As James Knowlson summarized it in his *Damned to Fame: The Life of Samuel Beckett,* the play's "success was assured when it became controversial." The critical and popular enthusiasm, though not universal, was widespread, and the production ran for four-hundred performances before moving to a larger theatre in Paris.

This process whereby ambivalence to the play ultimately evolved into popular and critical success was repeated when the play moved to London in August of 1955 for its first production using Beckett's English translation. Opening in a small "fringe" theatre (London's version of Off Broadway), "the play created an instant furore," according to Alan Simpson, writing in 1962, and quoted in Ruby Cohn's 1987 compilation, *Waiting for Godot: A Casebook*. Simpson added mat "[a]lmost without exception, the popular press dismissed it as obscure nonsense and pretentious rubbish. However, it was enthusiastically championed by Harold Hobson and Kenneth Tynan" (two of the most influential drama critics in London) and the play once again became controversial and thereby successful, eventually moving to a West End theatre (London's Broadway) and a long run. In February of 1956 an unsigned review in the London *Times Literary Supplement* by distinguished author G.S. Fraser asserted that die play was clearly a Christian morality play. This essay led to weeks of spirited exchange in the *Times* with some critics countering that the play was anti-Christian, others that it was Existentialist, and others that it was something else altogether. Characteristically, Beckett was mystified by the controversy, saying, according to Knowlson, "why people have to complicate a thing so simple I can't make out."

The first American production of the play, on the other hand, was quite uncomplicated; it was an unmitigated disaster. In January of 1956, director Alan Schneider opened what was to be a three-week preview run of the play in Coral Gables, Florida, near Miami, with popular comic actors and personalities Bert Lahr and Tom Ewell in the lead roles. As Schneider recounted (as quoted in Ruby Cohn's 1967 compilation, *Casebook on Waiting for Godot),* the production was a "spectacular flop. The opening night audience in Miami, at best not too sophisticated or attuned to this type of material and at worst totally misled by advertising billing the play as 'the laugh sensation of two continents,' walked out in droves. And the so-called reviewers not only could not make heads or tails of the play but accused us of pulling some sort of hoax on them." The production did not even finish the three week preview run, but months later the production did move to Broadway, with a new director and cast (retaining only Bert Lahr as Estragon). In New York, producer Michael Myerberg took a new tack on pre-production publicity, this time asking in his advertisements for an audience of "seventy thousand intellectuals." This time the production was a success, though still drawing divided opinions from critics and audience. The show ran for over 100 performances and sold almost 3,000 copies of the play in the theatre lobby.

There have been so many important productions of *Waiting for Godot* in our century that it is difficult to even list, much less summarize, them. An all-black production of the play on Broadway ran for only five performances late in 1956, with Earle Hyman as Lucky. There was a West Berlin production early in 1975 that Beckett himself directed. In a production in 1976 in Cape Town, South Africa, waiting for Godot seemed to suggest waiting for the end of apartheid. In 1984 there was a San Quentin Drama Workshop production involving Rick Cluchey, former inmate of San Quentin and audience member of the famous 1957 San Quentin production of the play. In 1988 Beckett went to court in an attempt to stop an all-female Dutch production, believing as he did that the characters in *Waiting for Godot* were distinctively male (Beckett and his lawyers lost in court). Also in 1988 there was a production at Lincoln Center in New York City, in which Estragon and Vladimir were played by well-known contemporary comedians Robin Williams and Steve Martin.

According to Martin Esslin in his *The Theatre of the Absurd, Waiting for Godot* had been seen by over a million people within five years after its first production in Paris and by the late 1960s had been translated into more than twenty languages and performed all over the world. Audiences coming to it without an awareness of its nature or history are perhaps still baffled by it, but the play can no longer be dismissed as it was by *Daily News* contributor John Chapman, one of its first New York critics, who, as quoted by the *New Republic's* Eric Bentley, called *Waiting for Godot* "merely a stunt."

Sources

Anouilh, Jean. Review in *Arts Spectacles,* February 27-March5, 1953, p. 1.

Bentley, Eric. Review in *New Republic,* May 14, 1956, pp. 20-1.

Ben-Zvi, Linda. *Samuel Beckett,* Twayne, 1986.

Blin, Roger. "Blin on Beckett," *Theater,* Fall, 1978, pp. 90-2.

Cohn, Ruby, editor. *Casebook on "Waiting for Godot,"* Grove, 1967.

Cohn, Ruby, editor. *"Waiting for Godot": A Casebook,* Macmillan, 1987.

Conner, Steven, editor. *"Waiting for Godot" and "Endgame": Samuel Beckett,* St. Martin's, 1992.

Esslin, Martin. "The Absurdity of the Absurd" and "Samuel Beckett: The Search for the Self," in his *The Theatre of the Absurd,* revised edition, Doubleday, 1969, pp. 1-65.

Hall, Peter. Extract from an interview on *Third Programme,* British Broadcasting Company (BBC), April 14, 1961. Reprinted in *"Waiting for Godot": A Casebook,* edited by Ruby Cohn, pp. 30-1, Macmillan, 1987.

Kenner, Hugh. *A Reader's Guide to Samuel Beckett,* Syracuse University Press, 1996.

Knowlson, James. *Damned to Fame: The Life of*

Samuel Beckett, Simon & Schuster, 1996.

Lemarchand, Jacques. Review in *Figaro Litteraire,* January 17, 1953, p. 10.

Zegel, Sylvain. Review in *Liberation,* January 7, 1953.

Further Reading

Bloom, Harold, editor. *Samuel Beckett's "Waiting for Godot,"* Chelsea House, 1987.

> Part of the Modern Critical Interpretations Series, this collection of modern critical commentary is designed for the college undergraduate.

Fletcher, John and Beryl S. *A Student's Guide to the Plays of Samuel Beckett,* Second Edition, Faber and Faber, 1985.

> Most valuable to the student because the book's section on *Waiting for Godot* includes notes explaining especially important or difficult details in the text of the play.

Gussow, Mel. *Conversations with and about Beckett,* Grove Press, 1996.

> A collection of transcriptions and interviews, some involving Beckett —who generally refused to talk about himself and his work in public —others involving his artistic collaborators.

Schlueter, June, and Brater, Enoch. *Approaches to Teaching Beckett's "Waiting for Godot,"* MLA, 1991.

A rich and varied collection of teachers' approaches to teaching the play, valuable for students as well.

Worth, Katharine. *"Waiting for Godot" and "Happy Days": Text and Performance,* Macmillan, 1990.

Focusing on the play as a text for theatrical production, this book is aimed specifically at the senior high school and college undergraduate reader, discussing both traditional views of the play and its continued relevance.

Lightning Source UK Ltd.
Milton Keynes UK
UKHW052303230519
343199UK00016BA/850/P